I Opened the Gate, Laughing

Mayumi Oda

I Opened the Gate, Laughing

An Inner Journey

Text by *Stephanie Guyer-Stevens*
Design by *Jenny Wunderly*

New Village Press • New York

Designed by Jenny Wunderly
Artwork by Mayumi Oda
Printed in China

20th Anniversary Edition
Published by New Village Press
New York, New York
New Village Press is a nonprofit, public-interest publisher.
www.newvillagepress.org

Distributed by New York University Press

Publication date: April 2024

Cataloguing available through Library of Congress
ISBN 978-1-61332-232-1

To my sons, Zachary and Jeremiah

Contents

Preface

At a certain point, I realized the life I was leading was not right for me, and I decided to live truer to myself.

I was thirty-eight years old when I separated from my husband after seventeen years of marriage. My husband, John Nathan, was a professor of Japanese Literature at Princeton University, and making a documentary film about Japan. I was an established professional artist. We both maintained exciting professional lives in New York City. Life was very exhilarating, but somehow it didn't make much sense to me. I felt very disconnected. John and I started to grow apart. I had run away from my family's values by becoming an artist, by marrying John, by joining the New York art world. Now I began to feel the urge to reconnect to that place of my childhood. It was no longer possible for me to live the life that I had been living.

Divorce was one of the most difficult things that I ever experienced. It was devastating to find myself in what was still a foreign country to me, and I wondered how we could create a good life. I tried to find a way to return to my own roots. I knew I couldn't return to Japan; it was no longer my home.

I was raised in a Buddhist family in Japan during and after World War II. My childhood revolved around seasonal Shinto rituals and Buddhist ceremonies. After the war, we were very poor and had very little material comfort, but as a child I didn't know any different. Living in the outskirts of Tokyo, surrounded by nature, I had a very rich life.

The Buddhist ethics of compassion were very important growing up in my family. My father, who was a Zen scholar, always told me that I had a Buddha nature, meaning that I could always find the person and the place within myself that I could trust. How could I find that place now?

In 1962 I entered the Tokyo University of Art. While I was a freshman there I met John, an American studying Japanese literature at Tokyo University. We married that same year. He was translating novels by Yukio Mishima and Kenzaburo Oe. I read many Japanese novels with him, and he taught me about American literature. He read me Faulkner's short stories at night, and I read Kerouac's *On the Road* by myself. We were very young, and we inspired each other.

After we both graduated in 1966, we moved to New York. I remember the day I left Japan for America. I stood at the Yokohama port wearing a yellow summer suit, leaning against my big American husband, feeling like a little canary chick leaving the mother's nest, to enter the world unknown.

When I became pregnant, my quest for the goddesses began. My small body was changing every day to give birth, and I had a strong urge to create large-breasted female figures. I was making etchings, and from the black aquatint background, goddesses emerged.

I gave birth to a son, Zachary Taro, in 1967. Imagining the world he would grow up in, I felt discouraged. We were in the

middle of the Vietnam War. I needed a talisman, some symbol of hope and encouragement. My prints of goddesses became like Neolithic fertility figurines, and I felt their strength when I made them. I knew that I had tapped into something very important.

When John received a fellowship from Harvard University, we moved to Cambridge, Massachusetts. My second son, Jeremiah Jiro, was born there in 1970. After taking care of two small boys and the house, very little time was left for me to create. I decided to build a printing studio in our basement and started to print silkscreen. Whenever I could steal time, during their naps or late at night, I ran downstairs to create goddesses. There, in the cold, dark basement during the long winter, I recovered that beautiful time I had spent with my mother in Iwate. Cherry blossoms on the riverbank, horsetails, young ferns, and even their smell appeared in my prints with intense colors. I dreamed of having a studio of my own out in the country.

In 1972, when John became a professor at Princeton, we moved to an old farmhouse that stood in the middle of a soybean field. I made the attic into my printing studio. I was in my mid-thirties. The urge to know myself became stronger, and I read many books on psychology, spirituality, and feminism. Having tried to get away from my own background for many years, I began to realize how important my Buddhist upbringing had been to me. With fresh eyes, I eagerly read Buddhist books for myself, not for my father's approval. Living in America, in a different culture, helped me to see my Japanese tradition with open eyes. It was like finding the door to a treasure house.

In 1978, Richard Baker Roshi, then abbot of the San Francisco Zen Center, invited us to spend the summer at Green Gulch Farm outside San Francisco. Life on the Zen farm felt so familiar to me, and it reminded me of how I had lived as a child. After John and I separated, I decided to live near Green Gulch farm, in Muir Beach, California, to practice Zen meditation.

In the process of searching for my own life, I rediscovered Buddhism, American style. Every day I sat in meditation for two hours. Zazen gave me a sense of routine that I clung to, that made my life functional. There, at Green Gulch Farm, my life was filled with the Three Treasures of Buddhism: Buddha, dharma, and sangha, which my family had always talked about and respected.

The Buddha we found in one another, practicing the awakening of our minds and living consciously. Through working in the garden, I felt the deep dharma moving through. We encountered impermanence and interconnectedness, nature's great teachings, as everyday truth. I found my sangha living among all my friends at Green Gulch Farm. There I was fortunate to experience the great blossoming of American Buddhism that was taking place at that time. Together we wholeheartedly dove into the experiment of living.

Years later, when I began to write this book, I realized that I had come back to the garden to heal myself.

In everything I have done since, including becoming an antinuclear activist, I have found the inner resources on which I rely came from my years there. Everything I have done is in the service of Gaia's garden. That is why I wanted to write a book about those years and about Buddhist practice, a book that could inspire young people to find their own path to awakening, to find their own garden.

> *Tranquil is this realm of Mind*
> *Ever filled with Heavenly beings,*
> *Parks and many places*
> *with every kind of gem adorned,*
> *Precious trees full of blossoms and fruits,*
> *where all creatures take their pleasure.*
> *All the Gods strike Heavenly drums*
> *and evermore make music,*
> *Showering Mandarava flowers*
> *On the Buddha and his great assembly.*
> *My pure land will never be destroyed.*
>
> Lotus Sutra

This is the verse I chanted every day as a child. Although I could not fully understand its meaning, its image sank deeply into my imagination. This was the world I wanted to live in.

Across the River

In my earliest memory, I am two years old, crying in my crib, grabbing the wooden bars, as the first air-raid sirens pierced the quiet of our town. My father and grandfather dug a shelter, shaped like a big mole hole, under the water-lily pond in our garden. Every time we heard the siren we ran into this hole. There, pressed up against one another, my mother tried to nurse my screaming baby brother, and my grandparents muttered a Buddhist mantra. We waited for a long time for the sirens to stop. From the opening of the dark hole, I watched the lights of B-29 bombers flying over our heads. Their blinking lights looked like evil eyes staring down at us, and I prayed that they wouldn't find us.

In March 1945 there was another big air raid on Tokyo. Bombers filled our sky and dropped their bombs from one edge of our city to the other. Like a carpet unrolling, fire swallowed a good part of the city. Even our suburban house faced great danger. My family decided that the time had come to evacuate the children and my mother to the safer countryside. My grandparents stayed in Tokyo to take care of our home and my father, who was teaching at the Naval Academy.

Grandpa packed my small knapsack with my crayons and my small porcelain mamagoto playhouse set, wrapping each thing neatly in newspaper. On the day of the spring equinox we left for the north, to the Iwate Prefecture, where my aunt had already moved. I carried the sack on my back, and Grandpa carried me on his back as we made our way to the terminal. I was afraid I'd never see him again and I cried hard. As we waved good-bye, he walked along with the train to the end of the platform and stood there. I leaned out the train window watching him becoming smaller and smaller, until finally the train took a sharp curve and he disappeared.

All the major cities in Japan were being bombed. But the war seemed far away from the northern country town where we were living. A big river ran through the valley beneath us. In the distance, over a long wooden bridge, stretched the green mountains of Iwate, topped with patches of snow. With crayons from my knapsack, my mother showed my cousins and me how to draw mountains. She drew the outline with brown, then filled the space with many trees of light and dark green. She told us to look at the mountain carefully as we drew.

Spring came all at once in the north. The peach, cherry, and apple trees blossomed together. We hiked to the riverbank and picked horsetails and wild chives. On the hill we gathered young ferns and butterbur sprouts. My mother picked stems of wild sorrel, peeled the skin, and gave them to me. I sucked the sour juice while I walked home.

The white apple blossoms on the hills turned orange in the setting sun, and the crows rushed toward the mountain to their nests. We felt happy and safe. We sang a song about the crow who left seven chicks nestling on the mountain.

One day we received a letter from my grandmother. She told us that worms had eaten the roots of one of the tomato plants in our garden, and that they were having a very hot summer. I missed my father and grandparents in Tokyo. I worried about their safety and felt bad that we were having such a good time in Iwate.

We left Iwate on the day of the autumn equinox to return to Tokyo.

After a long journey, we were home. Tokyo was gone. It had been reduced to a heap of rubble. My family had lost everything in the war except the house and the yard, but we were grateful that nobody in the family had been killed. My grandfather was in the garden weeding, and my grandmother welcomed us, only able to offer us hot or cold water. I drank fresh cold water from the well.

For a few years we had very little to eat. Some months we
had only sweet potatoes. My mother started to take her beautiful
kimonos to nearby farmers in exchange for rice. My grandparents made our Japanese garden into a vegetable patch. All the
adults were so busy with survival that we children were often
left alone. We did not have any toys except wooden blocks that
we had saved from before the war. We mostly played outside.

We also studied outside. My elementary-school days were
quite chaotic. There were not enough classrooms, so many class-
es were held outside and called Blue Sky Classrooms. I remember my afternoon math class under the wisteria trellis. I could
not concentrate on multiplication tables. I just sat there watching
the flower petals being blown by the May wind.

A persimmon tree covered the backyard. When I felt sad
and lonely, I used to climb the tree and put my arms around its
trunk. Sometimes the tree felt more like a mother to me than
my real mother. It was always there when I needed it. In spring
it blossomed with fragrant, white flowers with pointed petals like

folded origami. In autumn when the tree lost its leaves it was covered with orange persimmons whose weight bent the branches. All the neighborhood children climbed our tree and feasted on its bright fruit. It seemed the sweetest thing that we had ever tasted.

Atsuko, the girl next door, and I would play house under the tree. We spread a straw mat on the sunny side of the garden, and there we set up our kitchen. Seasonal flowers became our pretend food. We unraveled the grainlike amaranth flowers for red rice and served yellow chrysanthemum omelettes on plates made of camellia leaves. We squeezed purple-colored juice out of the morning glories. Time passed slowly.

We walked to the river to catch crayfish for our meals, but when we caught catfish we let them go, because we believed their whiskers would warn us of earthquakes. We floated bamboo- leaf boats downstream with a crew of poor ant sailors.

We girls picked flowers from the turned rice fields. The pink and white clover had a sticky sweet smell, and their shapes resembled the great lotus flower. We braided them into garlands and placed them on our heads. We never picked the dandelions, though, because they wilted easily, and we preferred to see them shining under the sun. Holding hands in a circle, we sang old folk songs.

Open, Open, What flowers were opened?
Lotus flowers opened.
When we thought they were open,
They were already closed.
Closed, Closed, What flowers were closed?
Lotus flowers closed,
When we thought they were closed,
Lotus flowers were already opened.

We sang this song over and over, opening and closing our circle. We imagined each of us becoming big lotus petals. Years later,

remembering this song, I realized that the lotus symbolized the purity and opening of the Buddha nature in each of us.

I often came back home in the middle of evening service. My grandparents would be sitting in the dark altar room with candles flickering and incense burning, repeating a Buddhist mantra, "Nanu Myo Horengekyo, Nanu Myo Horengekyo," which is about paying homage to the great lotus sutra. They believed this mantra would lead us to liberation from our suffer-ing. They asked me to join them, and I usually did. I liked the smell of incense; it made me feel calm.

Each November, there was a special rite-of-passage celebration, called Shichi Go San, "seven five three," for children of seven, five, and three years of age. The children would go to the shrine to report on their health and to be blessed with future prosperity.

When I was seven years old, my grandmother sewed a special silk kimono for me with a pattern of camellia flowers. My uncle, who had just returned from Java, cut my bangs straight across my forehead. He whispered to me that I would be a beautiful woman when I grew up. My mother tied a wide, pink silk bow around my small head.

All dressed up and feeling solemn, I walked with my mother to the shrine. The high-pitched note of a sho flute filled the shrine grounds. Children in colored silk kimonos waited their turn to receive the blessing. The shinto priest shook a duster made out of white paper over my head a few times to brush off the evil spirits and purify me, and I offered him a green sakaki tree branch. The leaves smelled so fresh, and I felt the sprit of the tree was present.

Bending my head down, all I could see were the red *haka-ma*, the long culottes of the miko girls who served at the shrine. But in the dim light, deep behind the center of the altar, I saw a round mirror on the cloud-shaped pedestal that I knew was a figure of Amaterasu, the Sun Goddess. I felt a strong connection to her, and I asked her to help me. In return, I promised to be a good girl.

Green Gulch Farm

I first visited Green Gulch Farm on my way to Tokyo in 1978. After many years of terrible drought, the California hills were so dry they looked like golden domes. I drove up the winding mountain road and looked down at the farm from the road above. Nestled in the bosom of gentle, sloping hills, it reminded me of a traditional Chinese landscape painting of paradise. Bean-sized people and horses were scattered in deep green fields.

Before he died, Shunryu Suzuki Roshi, the founder of the San Francisco Zen Center, asked Richard Baker to look for a farm near San Francisco to make a community where laypeople could practice Buddhism and live a simple life. Baker Roshi found Green Gulch Farm. In spite of the community's reluctance to take on such a large responsibility, Richard was convinced that Green Gulch would become a very important place for Buddhist development in America. Laypeople and families with children could live together to practice Buddhism daily. Visitors could come to discover Zen Buddhism for themselves.

People worked hard fundraising, turning the hay barn into a meditation hall, building houses, and cultivating the land. After many years of hard work, Green Gulch established a retreat and guest program as well as an organic farm.

One hot summer Sunday, I attended a lecture in the barn, which now housed a spacious meditation hall. Baker Roshi had returned from Tassajara Monastery, which was threatened by a big fire in the mountains of San Pedro National Forest. He talk-ed about how the monks were fighting the forest fire there, and how the cultivation of a calm mind was beneficial for this kind of task.

Especially because of the summer drought, the compost toi-let in the barn impressed upon me the community's respect for the land. Lavender and other herbs were hung from the ceiling to dry. It was like being inside a Japanese country temple, and I felt a keen attraction to the way people lived on this farm.

The year following our trip to the farm we lived in Tokyo. The frantic and fragmented city life of Tokyo and my own confusion made me miserable. I was no longer comfortable in my own country. It was as if I had become an oversized tatami mat that no longer fit into the immaculate tearoom. I had grown up differently from my friends in Japan.

I was also beginning to realize, sadly, that my husband and I were on different paths. I felt that John was pursuing life outwardly in his successful career, and I became increasingly interested in my internal life. We no longer had the same values.

I began practicing at the Zen Temple in Tokyo. But the temple was quite a disappointment to me. Women were not allowed to sit inside the meditation hall. The monks acted like Samurai robots. There, time seemed to have stopped many centuries ago. I thought I could even see invisible cobwebs all over the temple.

I often thought about that peaceful Zen farm I had visited in California. One day I dreamed I was living at the farm. In my dream my studio stood in the middle of a green field leading to the ocean, and the fields were covered with yellow squash blossoms.

John moved with us to California, but we decided to live apart. My two sons and I moved to a house in Muir Beach, near Green Gulch Farm. Zachary was eleven and Jeremiah was eight. In the yard stood a big walnut tree, which reminded me of the persimmon tree that had once covered our family's backyard in Tokyo. I knew that this was a safe place for my sons to grow up.

Under the walnut tree, my sons would play: climbing, swinging on the branches, hanging a dartboard and a sandbag for boxing, making a fort. Many kinds of birds visited the tree. In the morning sun, its shadows fell across my studio floor. The silver bark shone and the branches swayed in the wind. Children's voices echoed through the surrounding alder wood. I felt safe and protected, as if the tree spirit Yakshi was there with her round bosoms and forearms, holding us. It was like the way I used to feel under that big persimmon tree.

Still, it was a difficult time, since I was separating from John. For the first time in my life, I found myself living alone with my two sons. I was very sad, yet I also felt ready to know who I was. In my studio I sat for many hours watching the shadow of the walnut tree and my own breath, asking myself, "Am I all right?"

Once in a while the woodpeckers' pecking interrupted me, and I remembered I had work to do.

Single Mother's Zen Practice

Fragrant waters flow separately, with limitless colors.
Scattered about are all kinds of flowers, jewels, and sandalwood.
The myriad lotuses, in full bloom, are arrayed like robes.
Rare grass grows in net-like profusion and releases sweet perfume.

Limitless, boundless great Bodhisattvas,
Carrying canopies and burning incense, fill the Dharma realm,
Sending forth all kinds of wonderful sounds,
As they universally turn the Thus Come One's Dharma wheel.

from Flower Ornament Sutra

My housemate, Teresa, and I would wake up every morning at 3:30 A.M., when it was still deep night. We would put on our black sitting robes and hurry to the farm for 4:00 A.M. meditation.

As we walked along the creek, opening and closing the
many gates of the fields, a dark silence permeated the valley.
The work-horses sometimes frightened us with their loud, hot
breath, and owls perching on the electric wires flew away. On
stormy nights, strong winds from the angry ocean blew through

the gulch as if nature's big brush were stroking it, and we huddled close to each other, clutching our single umbrella tightly.

Each day we noticed the changes of the moon. When it was full we could walk without a flashlight. Under the pouring white moonlight, the surrounding bare hills lay motionless like sleeping dinosaurs.

We entered the meditation hall, which was called the Zendo. It was often very cold, without any heating. Facing the white, stark wall, about forty people would sit together in lotus position, feeling their breath going in and out. My crossed knees hurt a lot. Sometimes my spine was screaming. But after sitting for two hours, I always felt my cloudy mind become clearer, as if muddy water were settling the silt in the bottom of a bottle.

When we came out of the dark meditation hall after two hours of zazen, my heart was calm and my eyes were open. The world around us was awake. The sun had risen above the hill, making the whole valley glitter. We rushed back home through a sea of lettuce and cabbage, listening to the birds and frogs chirping, to make breakfast for our children. Then we went our separate ways, since Teresa lived in the main part of the house and I lived in the studio. There, I sat at the morning table with my sons and poured tea. Three of us were here, not four. John had been such a large presence in our lives. Our family felt small without him. The boys did not talk much, and watching them eat so strangely quiet, I felt a sharp pain.

The house belonged to the Zen Center of San Francisco. I lived there with three other single mothers, and between us we had eight children. We shared the chores and took care of one another's children as our own. It was lovely to watch them all piled up together over the torn-up couch in the living room, watching TV or playing cards together.

Yet despite my sense of belonging at the farm, I still was crushed by the idea that I could not keep our family together. I was not the good Japanese woman who stays with her husband till she dies. I felt I was betraying my sons and my parents.

Many times I felt like a failure at living my life.

Many people lent me some of their strength during this diffi-cult period, especially Teresa. She worked as a waitress at Greens Restaurant, which the Zen Center had just opened in San Francisco, and she was raising three teenage children alone. I saw her on her day off sitting in the sun, quietly peeling apples or pears. She was Spanish, and her sculpted face reminded me of an early Picasso painting of a woman with almond-shaped eyelids. Teresa was a master of enjoying the ordinary moment. Nothing seemed to faze her much. When, after experiencing numbness in her feet and hands, she was told by her doctor that she might have multiple sclerosis, she did not seem very upset. She took up yoga and swimming, and went on leading her life as usual.

Our children played in the fields, sliding down the dry grassy hills on cardboard, swimming in the ocean, fishing for trout and rock cod. Sometimes they came back home with a big catch and we cooked the fish.

I remember one evening especially well. The children came back home long after dark, their faces cold and red, noses running, and with tremendous pride, presented me with a huge deer antler they had found on the hillside. They were totally absorbed in their find. My sons told me, "Mommy, don't move from here. We like it here."

I planted daffodil bulbs under the walnut tree, turned over the soil for spring gardening, and went to the fields to paint. There, cabbage and lettuce spread their leaves, revealing mandalas of the field. Under the fog, the bright green lettuce leaves looked more beautiful than roses and peonies. My heart still pounds with the mystery of this blossoming out of wet, black soil.

My favorite vegetable was the purple cabbage. As if refusing the embrace of the big silver-violet leaves, the magenta core curled so tightly it reminded me of my own lonely heart. Even when I felt despair and sadness in those early days, painting the unfolding shapes and luminous colors of these vegetables gave me strength.

Near the ocean, vegetables whose colors are close to the colors of the sea grow very well. Kale, broccoli, and spinach reflect the turquoise blue of the water. Cauliflower is the white coral. Dewdrops on the leaves are like a crystal rosary scattered over the vegetable beds.

Buddhafields

On April 8 we celebrate Buddha's Birthday with the Flower
Festival. Adults and children at the farm gather flowers from the
hills and fields and decorate a small pagoda. We tile the roof
with magnificent roses and camellias and drape it with clusters
of wisteria, then the pagoda is placed in the center of the lawn.
The procession of children comes out pulling a small elephant
cart filled with wildflowers.

Under the flowered roof, the small statue of baby Buddha
stands in a bowl of sweet tea, pointing his right finger to heaven,
his left to the earth. When he was born, Buddha immediately
took seven steps forward and seven backward. Then he pro-
claimed, "On heaven and earth I am the world-honored one."
We offer him a shower of sweet tea with small bamboo ladles.
To celebrate his birth as a human baby surrounded by nature,
the monks recite the names of the flowers strewn around us:

Footsteps-of-spring, columbine, poppy, elderberry, lupine, sheep sorrel, buttercup, mustard, blackberry, filigree, winebark, wild cucumber, fringe cups, snakeroot, wild oats, larkspur, cow parsnip, Douglas iris, yellow paintbrush, forget-me-not, thimbleberry, thistle, woodmint, morning glory, bracken fern, milkmaids, foxtail, money plant, coast live oak, twinberry, wild onion, poison oak, shooting star, white iris, vetch, clover, miner's lettuce, woodland star, wild radish, Indian paintbrush, pearly everlasting, English plantain, burr clover, goldback fern, baby-blue-eyes, hazelnut, scarlet pimpernel, blue-eyed grass, cudweed, California sage, wild strawberry, sticky monkey flower, clinging bedstraw, polypody, ceanothus, wild geranium, lotus, wild currant,anemone, stock, carnation, calendula, blue iris, calla lily, lilac, sweet william, wallflower.

Then the pageant starts. The story of the birth of Siddhartha, Shakamuni Buddha, is celebrated. The beautiful masks of the Golden Buddha and his mother Maya, a six-tusked white elephant, demons, ribbons, scarves, and colored umbrellas all dance together to songs and drum sounds. A green dragon is lifted into the sky by colorful helium balloons.

As I watch this festival here in America, I can hear the familiar sweet voice of the daughter of the temple priest, reading to us children who gathered around her under the dark temple room. It was the same story of the birth of Buddha, and the story was written on the backsides of the big picture cards she held. With each episode she flipped the sheet, and we listened and watched this story every year, drinking sweet tea and eating rice cakes.

On the Fourth of July, the farm held a picnic. People harvested new potatoes, forking them from the soil carefully so as not to hurt them. The yellow finn and pinkish rose fir potatoes appeared as if by magic from the earth. The children got very excited and stuck their hands into the soil to find them. Then we baked the new potatoes over a charcoal grill set out in the field, and waited around it impatiently. The smell and taste of these potatoes brought us such satisfaction, we felt we were part of this earth.

One morning, I stood in the middle of a lettuce patch. Staring at the soft green color, I thought, "They came out of the earth," then something struck me with great force. They were all alive . . . so alive, breathing just like us. I felt we were all part of the great life force. I started to cry. I was so completely supported by this earth.

After the long growing season comes Thanksgiving. The color- ful harvests from the field—broccoli, cauliflower, green and purple cabbage, pink and yellow potatoes, orange pumpkins, many kinds of lettuce, magenta beets, carrots, and bouquets of herbs—are offered on the altar, a cornucopia of Buddha's field.

The whole community is invited to celebrate with a scrumptious vegetarian feast. Vegetable crudités with herb dip are the hors d'oeuvres. Pumpkin soup is served in its own shell, then hearty nut loaves come with creamy mashed potatoes, cranberry sauce, and pungent gravy. Pumpkin pies are baked with Hokkaido squash; their chestnutlike flavor makes the pies very rich.

We receive so much from this earth. She is our mother who
holds us with such fecundity, and we truly feel deep gratitude
for her gift.

> *Innumerable labors brought us this food.*
> *We should know how it comes to us.*
> *Receiving this offering*
> *We should consider whether our virtue and practice deserve it.*
>
> *We venerate all the great teachers*
> *and give thanks for this food:*
> *The work of many people*
> *and the suffering of other forms of life.*
>
> (From a meal blessing)

One breakfast during a retreat I took a mouthful of hot
oatmeal, and suddenly tears filled my eyes. I felt so fortunate to be
sitting there, tasting this spoonful of nourishment. My experience

in that moment was the gift of so many people. For 2,500 years Buddhism has been passed on. The great teachers carried it from India to China, to Japan, and then to America. For centuries people have sat many long retreats. Like us, they sat in silence, watched their breath going in, going out, meeting their own minds and hearts.

John was taking care of our sons. Many people had worked hard taking care of the buildings, turning this barn into a meditation hall. The cooks had been up since 4:00 A.M. to prepare this meal. Farmers worked hard for this food. The fields and sun and rain—my connection to all of them was endless. I felt I sat in the center of a mandala, like a golden Buddha receiving these tremendous innumerable gifts. I sat in the center of the world of interdependence, eating oatmeal.

Flood

After several years of drought we at last had a long rainy winter. Ten days of uninterrupted rain made the valley swell like a wet sponge, and on a morning of the full moon, when coastal tides rose, our house was completely flooded. Water gushed down from the hills like an angry white dragon. We had about one hour to move our furniture. We put everything we could lift onto the second floor and pulled out the wall-to-wall carpeting. I packed the boys' clothes and my Green Tara statue and we evacuated to the temple. The garden became one big pond, and water entered my bare studio, from doors and electric outlets, penetrating everywhere. I was awed at how small we humans are in comparison to nature's force and realized that we can never go against it.

When it was over, it took many months to make our house livable, though I didn't mind so much. I felt as if some change

was happening inside of me, too. I cleaned the layers of mud and threw away the things that I had been carrying around.

I realized how deeply I loved John, who had brought me to America, taught me English, and supported me in becoming an artist. My life had been so inseparable from his; it was as if we had been Siamese twins. But, without our even noticing, our paths had diverged until finally we had to let ourselves be separate.

I was still very sad, but I felt strength inside my body. I knew I could stand alone. The water had washed away some of my grief, too, as if purifying me, and the flood left a dark, fertile silt in the garden, out of which golden daffodils blossomed with great intensity. I painted the image of Green Tara emerging from the cabbage field.

Nettle Soup

From the beginning, I felt very close to Harry Roberts. His hefty yet comfortable body reminded me of the figure in the photograph of my maternal grandfather, who had died long before I was born.

Harry was part Yurok Indian, though he looked more like a big Irishman to me. He was raised by a Yurok uncle, Robert Spott, and trained as a high medicine man. He was also a master fisherman and lumberjack, a turquoise trader, a cowboy, a horticulturist, and an expert in soils and geology. He had been a dancer as well, and used to dance with Ginger Rogers. He once showed me the shining black dancing shoes he had kept from that time.

Harry stayed in the house closest to mine along the creek. My neighbor Yvonne Rand had given him a room to live in when he became very ill. By his bedside was a small woodstove, and he would show me how to make a fire with wet wood. I watched him carefully. He tore the newspaper into strips and placed them on the ash, then piled the dry twigs and the wet wood on top. He did all this in a few minutes. When he lighted the match the wood caught fire immediately and burned as if the chimney was sucking the air.

After the winter rains, nettles grew all over our backyard. Their leaves were covered with stinging furs. Harry taught me how to make nettle soup. He told me to put rubber gloves on and pick the tender top leaves. I cooked them with potatoes and leeks. He sat in his bed eating my thick soup, telling me, "It's good, good medicine for spring." Every spring I make nettle soup, and the smell of the green leaves reminds me of Harry.

My sons were city kids, so Harry decided they should take a four-day raft trip down the Russian River. They bought thick, fatty beef sticks, made a pile of carrot and celery sticks, and froze cartons of milk to put in their cooler. Then Harry taught them how to catch turtles, using bundles of twigs and leaves on their heads for camouflage. Harry said to them, "Make sure you guys bring back turtles for my soup." They never caught any turtles, but the river trip became an annual event.

With his simple way of going through daily life, Harry was a teacher to many people. I was sorry that I couldn't give him more time. When I apologized, he comforted me, saying, "It's good for some people to take care of others. But you, take good care of your boys."

That winter it rained a lot, and his bones hurt him. One afternoon when I was giving him a massage, he asked me to sing him a song, so I sang Japanese lullabies from my childhood. He said, "They sound just like ours," and then like a child he fell asleep and began to snore.

One of Harry's great teachings was that we should open our eyes and believe what we see, being simply and deeply observant. Harry had a special way of observing nature. Yvonne usually drove him in his yellow Ford pickup, "Marigold," going very slowly so he could see the things around him. He walked slowly on his crutches around the yard and the alder woods, stopping frequently to look around. Pointing at the hills he said, "Those big rocks over the highway weren't showing when I first came here. The land is eroding fast." He had been a cowboy in this valley in the 1930s. His dream was to reforest the entire area, and he was quite sad that perhaps there would be no one to carry out his teachings and his vision.

Several months before Harry died, Masanobu Fukuoka visited the farm. A Japanese farmer, philosopher, and teacher, he is the author of a book, *One-Straw Revolution*, about his life-long exploration of natural farming. When Harry and Mr. Fukuoka met, they understood each other as if they were long-lost friends. Yvonne drove Marigold to nearby Muir Woods to show Mr. Fukuoka a primeval redwood forest.

Mr. Fukuoka told Harry that the way redwoods grow here in Muir Woods very much resembles the Yaku cryptomeria forests in Japan. He thought cryptomeria trees might in fact suit the eroded soil here better than the original redwoods do now, since cryptomeria have a deeper root system than redwoods. When Fukuoka went home to Shikoku, he sent Harry a small Bodhi-dharma carved from Yaku cryptomeria, which Harry kept at his bedside until his death. Along with the figure came a package of cryptomeria seeds. The envelope was addressed to "American Guardian." Harry sent him a bowl carved of redwood in return.

On the full moon a month before Harry died, he planted these seeds in a flat as he lay in his bed, surrounded by his students. He told them that these seeds were Fukuoka's spirit, and he asked them to please take care of them. On Arbor Day at the farm Harry said, "Remember: Buddhism is forever. It is not a crash program for the next five weeks. We are looking at things from the perspective of five hundred years. If we make it for five hundred years, then we will make it for five thousand. We are building for the far future." Then Harry planted many cuttings of black cottonwood trees from the Klamath River,

which people from the farm had traveled for three days and six hundred miles to get.

Harry died a few days before the spring equinox. Yvonne boiled wild Yerba Santa leaves that I had picked the previous summer on Mt. Tamalpais, and she washed his body with this tea. Before his death, Harry had made sure that the herb was picked in midsummer on this mountain. He lay beneath the open blossoms of the crab-apple tree, his large nostrils and mouth open like black holes. His hands were folded on his chest, holding the small bundle of a woodpecker feather and two dentalia shells wrapped in ermine fur. Dentalia shells were used by the Yuroks as money to pay the ferryman to take them across the river to the other shore, surprisingly like our Japanese custom of letting the dead carry six old pennies.

I watched the white petals falling from the crab-apple tree. He's gone, I realized, to the other shore. His death was complete and beautiful to me. Even in his death he was teaching us something important.

The cryptomeria seeds germinated in April, but Harry was gone. My friend Wendy held the flat for a long time and cried. In the summer, she transplanted the tiny seedlings into a deeper flat, and next year to a garden bed. We planted out about 130 cryptomeria on Arbor Day a few years later.

Five years after Harry's death, Mr. Fukuoka revisited the farm. Wendy showed him a photograph of Harry seeding cryptomeria from his bed. Mr. Fukuoka was deeply moved by Harry's strong desire for reforestation. When people took him to see the cryptomeria on the hill, the trees were already five and six feet tall, fenced by wire cages to protect them from deer damage. Mr. Fukuoka burst into tears.

Now I understood why I was here in California, practicing Buddhism with American and European friends. In Japan, Buddhism for me was like the dusty sutra books on the altar. Here it is alive, taking new form. The ancient Buddhist teaching of interconnectedness is enriched by the native

American tradition of reverence for the earth. I want to see the blossoming of this new hybrid flower, and I know that we at the farm were all part of this process.

Spirit of the Valley

The spirit of the valley is immortal.
It is called mysterious feminine
The gateway of mysterious feminine
Is called the root of heaven and earth.
It springs continuously.
Use never exhausts the source.

I call my house and studio Spirit of the Valley. The house is tucked into an alder grove along Redwood Creek, which traces its source from Mt. Tamalpais, the sacred healing ground for Miwok Indians for centuries. I hear that the herbs growing on this mountain are especially potent.

The creek runs through the ancient redwood grove, Muir Woods, through my garden and empties into the Pacific Ocean a half mile down from here. Coho and silver salmon come to spawn in Muir Woods in winter. Last year, after a big autumn storm, I watched the salmon, their silver bellies turned to bright red, swim upstream. Over the years I've received much caring and inspiration from this mountain.

It is often very cold here. When I first moved in, the house was damp and dark inside, like an old depressed soul. Then one day I received a vision during my meditation. My house was transformed into a very open, light, and glorious space. Painted pink with green trim, the house was sitting in the midst of a profusion of flowers. I heard a voice saying, "the House of the Goddess of the Valley." I wondered, Who is the Goddess of the Valley? Later, I remembered the name Spirit of the Valley from an ancient teaching of the Tao Te Ching. Mt. Tamalpais's rich soil and healing energy pour down into the valley, bringing much abundant life. I see the presence of mysterious feminine, Mother Tao, here in the valley, receiving and creating new life.

When the house went up for sale I bought it and started to renovate it. Steve Stucky, a former Green Gulch director, landscaped the garden. First we had to clean the yard. Many trees had fallen down during the heavy winter storms. An irrigation system was put in.

It was a great joy to take care of this old house. It gradually became light and cheerful and began to feel very feminine. Many people worked hard together, transforming the house. We ate lunch and shared tea every day for many months. The house still holds the energy of this original crew.

I wanted to have a home where I could live and work to-gether with friends, in harmony and good communication. I felt the need to have an extended family, for neighbors helping one another, sharing food and taking care of one another, the way we had lived when I was a child in the suburb of Tokyo right after the war. I wanted my sons to grow up in a big family household.

Four babies were born in this house: Mark, Joshua, Tajha, and Marea. I was happy to help the mothers during their pregnancies, and I took a part in the births, too. Mark and Tajha were born in our back bedroom. It felt right to receive

babies there, and the whole house felt sweet and soft with their presence. The babies loved to go out in to the garden. Especially when they were cranky, I used to take them out and sing Japanese children's songs.

> *Hush little Baby.*
> *Tomorrow is the forty-ninth day of your birth.*
> *We will all go to the shrine to pray.*
> *Hush hush little Baby.*
> *How should we pray in the shrine?*
> *Good health to you your whole life.*

The garden was so still that the babies usually fell asleep in my arms.

Several years later we opened the attic to extend it. I had a vision of the new space as a Japanese meditation tearoom. I was fortunate to have Sakaguchi-san, a skilled Japanese carpenter, working for me, along with two Korean Zen practitioners, Mushim and Sunbul, and together they made a beautiful tearoom. After it was finished, Mushim, a nun, and Sunbul, a monk, left, wearing gray monks' clothes, for Sue Doc Sa Mountain in Korea, the sacred place of the Chogei Zen order, for a long winter retreat.

One autumn day I sat alone in the big empty tearoom. Sun was pouring in from the skylight, making the tatami gold, and a scent of cedar and fresh grass from the tatami mats filled the room. Everything was quiet, except for the sound of fallen alder leaves scratching the rooftop. My two sons were grown up and had left home for art colleges. I felt strongly that my house was not meant just for my own use anymore. The idea came to me of offering the house as a place for retreats to explore creativity. The Spirit of the Valley was entering into the house. Since then I have held many such retreats to share the bountiful creative energy I have received from the Spirit of the Valley.

One year after the tearoom was built, Mushim came back from her retreat in Korea, pregnant. She had conceived the child at the top of Su Doc Sa Mountain. The father was the head monk there. She said, "It simply happened; the baby wanted to be born." She seemed distressed and needed a safe place to give birth, so I offered this house. I thought that the baby must be a very special child, maybe a Buddha baby, conceived as he was by monk and nun.

Mushim became my secretary, and we sat in meditation together every morning in the tearoom. She probably never thought that one day she would be back here sitting in the room she had helped to build. As so often before, I saw how life goes beyond our calculations.

Mushim would say with a smile, "I could not abort the baby, so I surrendered myself to fate. Now people are taking care of me." In early spring, we had a baby shower, and many friends brought gifts. One friend brought a beautiful bentwood rocking chair. Mushim's baby was born in April. Cathie, my studio assistant, and I helped with the birth at the hospital. Mushim named her baby boy Joshua.

We held a Buddhist ceremony to welcome Joshua, along with Mushim's family and friends. In the yard we dug a deep hole to bury the placenta. Over it we planted a small Golden Delicious apple tree, with the hope that Joshua would grow up like a big healthy tree. Everybody at the ceremony poured shovel-fuls of dirt into the hole.

One sunny afternoon in the living room, I watched Mushim rocking in her chair slowly, as Joshua sucked at her round breast. His face looked so peaceful, I was filled with joy.

Some mornings Joshua joined our sittings, lying between us. He especially liked the "Great Compassionate Dharani" chant, in Korean, a melodic chant that offers love and an open heart to every being. He seemed to remember it from when he was in his mother's belly.

Another friend who joined our household at a time of personal crisis was Dean Rolston. He had spent some summer months at the Tassajara monastery, and he owned an art gallery in SoHo in New York. When he became ill with AIDS he closed the gallery and came to the farm to stay. He wanted to work in the kitchen, but the kitchen director told him that this sort of work was unsuitable for a person with AIDS.

Dean was outraged. His face was swelling, and I was worried about his health, so Mushim and I talked over the possibility of having him come live in our house. Both of my grandparents and my parents had died at home, where my family took care of them. It seemed natural to have Dean at my house. A man facing death could live with new life. Because the baby was only six months old we were worried about the health consequences, but when we checked with doctors we were reassured that it was perfectly safe. I asked him, "Can you come here to live, not die?"

Baby Joshua imparted to us all a sweet, calm energy. It was wonderful to watch Joshua and Dean sitting together eating

oatmeal for breakfast. We meditated together whenever Dean
felt well enough to get up. He got up more and more often,
and he practiced yoga in the living room under the afternoon
sun. Some days he sat there quietly and worked on a novel. He
drove to the hospital by himself to receive chemotherapy, which
made him quite ill. But I never heard him complain.

Sometimes I made him chicken soup. He loved cooking and
we often entertained guests from the city with meals made from
our garden vegetables. When Dean became healthier, he cooked
the meals for our retreats.

Dean and I took the Bardo (Tibetan Book of the Dead)
teaching from Sogyal Rinpoche together. We sat around him
and listened to his teaching.

"We are all dying," Sogyal Rinpoche said and started to snap
his fingers, snap, snap, snap. *"Death, death, every second is death."*

Facing death, Dean never wasted time and lived every
day quite fully, appreciating the small details of life that nature

provides. Whenever he came back from a walk in the hills or on the beach, he was filled with love for nature and marveled over what he had seen, taking deep breaths. He was a great teacher for me. I learned to see things differently by living with him. One day he said, "You know, my white blood cell counts are so low that the doctor thinks I should be dead by now. Do you think this is a miracle?" I thought, and I said, "No. It is very natural, isn't it?"

After living with us for a year and a half, Dean felt strong enough to live by himself, and he moved into a warmer house up the hill in Muir Beach. He died several years later.

His ashes were returned to my house in a square box wrapped in green velveteen cloth. It sat at my altar for many months. After six months or so we finally did the Ashes Ceremony. We scattered some of his ashes, which really looked like bone meal that we use for gardening. The rest of them we took to the sea.

In the Garden

Form does not differ from emptiness.
Emptiness does not differ from form.
That which is form is emptiness.
That which is emptiness, form.

The soil is dark and full of dead leaves and worms. It smells like my grandmother's bed where we used to snuggle. Spring comes early here after the long winter rains. Crocuses, narcissus, and freesia shoot out their buds, and we await new blossoms every day. The crab apple's pink buds open to snow-white flowers, and monarch butterflies rest their tired and torn wings after their long journey from Mexico. An abundance of spring flowers—purple, maroon, and yellow bearded Iris, pink and mauve aqua-legia, and white dianthus—paint a beauty beyond imagination. These colors go right into my heart and dissolve into my whole being.

The kitchen garden is a special joy. I grow the usual vegetables like lettuce, kale, chard, rocket, leeks, garlic, pumpkins, snap peas, and string beans.

Potatoes are especially fun to grow. I love their nutty, earthy flavor. I put big pots of water on the stove to boil and then go out to the garden to pick the potatoes. I dig them from the sides of the plant with my hands, so they will keep producing all summer long. Fresh potatoes are tender and juicy; I scrub them lightly and slide them into the boiling pot. Boiled potato and chopped parsley with plenty of butter is one of the most divine foods that I know of. This was what my father wanted to eat every day when he visited here.

My family used to grow its own vegetables, too, in the backyard during and after the war. We were not good farmers, but we depended on that vegetable garden for our meals. My grandpa became very serious about production. He got up every morning, very early, to work in the garden. He took his calligraphy brush out, to pollinate the pumpkin flowers. He collected pollen from the male flowers and brushed it over each female flower. He was so meticulous about his work that we ate pumpkins that winter till we turned orange.

In my family's garden I loved to pick the ripened tomatoes. The dark green leaves gave out a strong smell, which I breathed in deeply. The tomatoes were red and warm from the sun; it felt like they were about to burst. My grandma put them in the icebox, and before serving them she peeled and sliced them, then sprinkled a little bit of the treasured sugar she had saved on them. I felt it was the most delicious thing I would ever taste.

In Muir Beach I had tried to grow tomatoes for several years, but the summer fog prevented them from ripening, and finally in the seventh year I gave up. I was disappointed but understood that the same fog makes lettuce and other leafy vegetables to grow tender and allows us to get fresh salad from our garden ten out of twelve months.

In summer, vegetables seem to grow before our eyes. After the full moon, swollen seeds germinate profusely, and zucchini and pumpkins grow like balloons. During the dry summer we need to conserve water, so all kinds of weeds are left in the garden for a green mulch, to keep in the moisture. Lavender, sage, and oregano release their strong aromas generously.

In autumn the alder loses its leaves and shows its bare branches. Through the lacelike grove, I can see the surrounding hills, and the animals come down from above to the greener valley. A red fox sits on the garden table. It reminds me of the stone figure of a fox shrine I used to visit as a child. A raccoon family makes a procession to the cat's food. Some nights, deer jump over the fence looking for soft vegetation to eat. Their thin elegant bodies shine under filtered moonlight, and their footsteps make crisp sounds over fallen leaves.

Sometimes I get lost watching insects at work. Bees, busy over the ink-blue borage flowers, collect pollen and make it into balls. Sometimes the balls grow almost too big for the bee to fly with. A tiny white spider weaves delicate hexagonal webs in the herb garden, moving her long thin legs as fast as she can and waiting for

prey. It is terrifying to watch her eat a fly still half-alive. She sucks
juice out of the body and then starts to nibble. Some mornings
I see dozens of nets stretching among the shrubs and flowerbeds,
dewdrops reflecting the sun. As I watch these tiny creatures and
their magnificent work, my sense of time slides into theirs, and
their small world expands into the big universe.

What does the garden do to us? I watch the plants germinate,
grow, blossom, make seeds, and wither, becoming soil, and come
back to grow again, and again. I realize that we are like them,
being born, crawling, walking, growing up, giving birth to new
life, and getting old and finally disappearing. The dharma wheel
turns and turns, creating, changing every moment, yet continuing.
Why do we think we are different from plants? Do plants die? Do
we really die? We came out of emptiness, and return to emptiness.
Being in the garden gives me a great feeling of rest.

One day while I was weeding, enjoying the quiet afternoon
sun, a small airplane suddenly flew very low overhead. I ducked

down and ran under the pear tree. My heart was beating very fast. In that moment the Coast Guard plane had become a B-29, dropping bombs on the street of my childhood, and my heart beat with the fear of fifty years ago.

When I realized that I was squatting in my peaceful garden I felt a great sense of relief, but I also felt sad that there are so many children who are suffering just like I did when I was small. Because of my painful experience, I can fully treasure the abundance of life. It is deeply comforting to live close to nature, to be part of the big cycle.

I knew that I had come back to Gaia's secret garden to nurture myself and my children. With a secure fence around me, I healed. I became whole.

The Deer's Path

One summer day when I went into the garden, I felt called by the creek. I put on long rubber boots and opened the gate to the woods. The stream was almost dry and showed its pebbly bottom, but some water was still running. I had forgotten how wonderful and mysterious it was in the woods. The trees seemed to absorb all the noise and craziness outside. The alders were as tall as seventy feet, making a high green canopy, and underneath grew buckeye trees, hung with silver lichen, and pungent laurel and elderberries. A fat gray owl flew across under the canopy and frightened me.

I waded down the creek bed and came upon a quiet, deep pool. I took my clothes off and plunged in. The water was ice cold and smelled like alder lye.

Floating, I noticed at the muddy corner of the pool many deer footprints, small and large, sliding into the water. A family of deer must come here to drink, I thought. The place felt sacred and protected and I even thought I could smell the musky scent of their bodies. I could see the path they used to come through the woods.

Then I realized I was following the path, through bushes, pushing aside ferns and prickly nettles, passing old fallen trees that were decaying and turning into soil. I was amazed how moist and soft the ground was. The path became narrow and low, and I had to bend down to walk through.

Suddenly I was on the other side of the fence. I saw my pink house in the distance. I stood there and saw my garden through a deer's eyes.

The garden that I loved so much looked ridiculous to me. It had the self-conscious stiffness of a proper English garden. And now in the summer heat it looked dry and completely alien from the wild green of the alder grove surrounding it, as though it did not belong in this mysterious valley at all. I was dumbfounded.

I had worked so hard, for seven years, making my own paradise, putting a fence around it to keep the deer away.

In this garden I had felt safe and protected. In this sanctuary I had sewn my torn pieces back together and found my wholeness. All these years I had been trying to re-create the exquisite moment of utter freedom that I felt as a child, across the river, in the field full of dandelions and clover. But now I had taken the deer's path and had seen the other side of my fence.

There were several gates around the fence. I opened them all. I felt energy from the woods and from everywhere pouring into my garden and into me. I was ecstatic. I did not need barriers to protect myself anymore. I started to laugh, hard, and ran into my garden, uttering "Thank you, thank you."

At that moment, my garden at Muir Beach became interwoven with that timeless playground of my childhood. The whole world became my garden.

I decided to take the fence down.

Acknowledgments

In the autumn of 1990 I spent a few months in Venice, Italy. I had gone there to have an exhibition and to lead workshops, and I stayed on, caught by the quietness and the beauty of the city. Sitting in the cafe at the side of the open market, I watched the vendors unloading vegetables and fruits from the boats: golden grapes and ripe figs; pomegranates, purple radicchios, warty pumpkins. Tables were laden with the fecundity of the earth.

I felt the need to reflect on my life at Green Gulch Farm Zen Center in California, so I started to write about it. When I finished writing, I didn't think to look for a publisher. I was writing this book for myself. I thought of it just as a process that I needed to go through to understand things that had gone on in my life. While writing, I began to realize that I had learned to love nature as my mother. I was ready to go out into the world in her service. I became an antinuclear activist, and the manuscript stayed unpublished.

Years later, I pulled out the manuscript and explored the possibility of writing a book about my years in the garden and about Buddhist practice. I met Stephanie Guyer-Stevens in Hawaii and gave her the manuscript. Together we found the real story in the text, and it blossomed into this book.

I decided to illustrate it with the drawings of all the flowers and vegetables that I made during those years in Green Gulch Farm, and in my garden. I talked to Michael Katz, my book agent, about my plan, and he suggested that we ask Jenny Wunderly to design it. I knew that Jenny was a wonderful abstract painter, but I did not know that she had previously worked as a graphic designer. I gave her a stack of artwork and the text, and asked her to design the book however she wanted. I loved what she surprised me with.

This work was no longer just my book; it became our book. It was a great joy to work with young women: Stephanie and

Jenny. Their fresh talent helped bring this book alive. I give them my deep thanks.

I am also very grateful to the community at Green Gulch Farm that gave me and my family comfort. I owe much to Richard Baker Roshi, who taught me American Zen. Without him I never would have returned to Buddhism.

I am filled with gratitude as I see the faces of a great many people with whom I shared my life at the farm: Ginnie, Renee, Yvonne, and their children; Lou and Blanche Hartman; Emilla, Michael, Betsy, and Ken; Meg and Mark; Jane and Frank; and Wendy and Peter.

So many people, some mentioned in this book, shared my house, Spirit of the Valley: Graham and Hideko and their son, Mark; other single mothers: Kay, Daya, Teresa, and their children; Ken and Taira; Heather and Sydney and their babies, who were born there; and Pauline and Barbara and Scott. Peter Kaufmann, my longtime boyfriend, provided us with the most beautiful piano music and with deep caring for my two sons.

Their lives have affected me deeply and helped me to unfold. Through them I learned to trust myself and others. I feel grateful to be living such a fortunate life.

I would also like to thank Layla Bockhorst, who helped me to type my original manuscript; Jane Hirshfield, who corrected my English; and Noel Oxhandler, Su Moon, and Linda Hess for editing my early edition. I also thank Nion McEvoy, who was then the young editor of my book at Chronicle Books.

Michael Katz came up with the title, *I Opened the Gate, Laughing*, and we shared a good laugh. Thank you, Michael, for your genius for making things happen. I hope that I can keep my gate open always.